T0158972

A Look Behind the Walls

Connie Alexander

Inspiring Voices®
A Service of **Guideposts**

Inspiring Voices books may be ordered through booksellers or by contacting:

Inspiring Voices
1663 Liberty Drive
Bloomington, IN 47403
www.inspiringvoices.com
1-(866) 697-5313

ISBN: 978-1-4624-0319-6 (sc)
ISBN: 978-1-4624-0318-9 (e)

Library of Congress Control Number: 2012916508

Printed in the United States of America

Inspiring Voices rev. date: 09/20/2012

CONTENTS

Special Thanks

I WOULD LIKE TO express my appreciation to the Lord for gifting me with Christian parents who raised me in a home full of His Love. My Mom and Dad introduced me to the importance of a relationship with Jesus by the way they lived and walked out their daily lives and still do. I Love You, Mom & Dad!

I would also like to Thank God for the blessing of my wonderful husband, Clayton. Clayton has shown me what it means to love with the unconditional love of Christ and has been a living example of how to step out in faith and follow Christ obediently. I Love You and Thank God for You "My Sweetie Boy"!

I.

A Look Back

As I LOOK back I have to admit that I never thought one spiritual weekend would have had such an impact on my life. Twenty years ago I attended a "Walk to Emmaus" (spiritual weekend). It was a wonderful experience of God's Love being showered on you all through the weekend. Probably the way we Christians are supposed to actually act everyday, but most of the time we don't. The funny thing was that I did not really desire to attend it. I was just going to check out what it was that caused such a change in my husband, Clayton. He had started going to men's morning Bible studies and some kind of a monthly fellowship meeting. It was not a bad change but there was definitely something different about him. I was almost convinced that he was in a cult and I needed to go investigate. I really had never thought of myself as having a "control issue"; however, I did insist on driving myself to the location for the weekend. About 3 hours away from our hometown on the way there I almost convinced myself that I had been to enough of these weekends that I could probably fake it. I considered checking into a motel and spending the weekend shopping. All I can tell you is that I am glad I did not follow through on that idea for a multitude of reasons. One of which was that I would have missed a beautiful blessing that has guided my adventures in life.

One of the personal decisions I made at that retreat was to rededicate my life to Christ. As a Baptist I had long ago quit "walking the isle" to rededicate my life because I had found that I would only fail, disappoint God again. I could never measure up to His standards; however, that weekend it was like God agreed with me. I would fail, but if I would let Him use me He had the power to succeed. Not me. Him. As for my part, I told Him that I was willing to be used by Him. At that point, I had no idea about the journey He was about to take me on.

My husband, Clayton, had been going out to the local prison and preaching for several months because the prisons were short of chaplains, and the local prison had just started operating a few months earlier. They were using local believers to minister to the inmates. I thought that it was just fine for my husband to do that, it just wasn't for me.

I did not have a clue about God's sense of humor. When Clayton approached Kerri Gandy, my singing partner, about the two of us going out and bringing some special music for him on Sundays at the prison, she jumped at the chance. I did not have a similar reaction. I politely told her she was crazy and "No I'm not going to do that!" But no sooner were the words out of my mouth than that tugging at my heart started, and it was as if God whispered, "I thought you told me at the retreat that you would go anywhere I provided you an opportunity." Now, when I made that decision at the retreat, I pretty much figured that God would provide opportunities in some of the small towns around West Texas. So, I had figured on singing at small churches on Sunday mornings. That was my plan.

Well, you guessed it, on Sunday we were at the prison. Kerri was all smiles and bursting with excitement. I almost hyperventilated when the doors were shut behind us. My pious, rebellious, resistant attitude of taking the Gospel "to the heathens" was quickly changed and the feeling of panic left as soon as I heard the first "man in white" (inmate) pray. It was clear that he was a lot closer to God at that point than I was. I know that we hear a lot about "jailhouse conversions", and talk about how fake or convenient it was for a prisoner to claim that God had changed his life; however, when I look back over my personal life experiences I have to admit that it was in my lowest times or darkest valleys that I cried out to God and earnestly began to seek Him. I believe that if all of my freedom was taken away and I was locked away I would begin to look for answers. So, I can see how men in the prison systems start to seek God or answers. On that Sunday, I began a journey of participating in prison ministry that Clayton had already begun. We have been active in prison ministry for almost twenty years.

We also started working in the Kairos Ministry. It is patterned after the "Walk to Emmaus" in that "free world" men enter the prison and present a short course in Christianity over a weekend to inmates who have indicated to the Chaplain an interest in attending. Most of them actually go for the cookies and the home cooked meals that they get during the Kairos.

These men are society's outcasts and have not felt loved by anyone in a long time. They have been locked away for long periods of time and most are forgotten as time moves quickly, passing them by. Don't get me wrong they are there for a reason, and I am not an advocate for opening the doors and releasing them all. Some of these "men in white" are not the person you want as a next door neighbor; however, they are individuals who eventually <u>will be released</u> back into society, and how they emerge from the prison will have a direct impact on our society. If they are treated poorly while inside, they will exit full of hate, bitterness, and go back into the same lifestyle that landed them in prison in the first place. If they are not provided opportunities to get an education or to learn a trade how can they be expected to start over in a society that does not want them? We don't want them working for us, living next to us, or even sitting next to us at church. Where exactly do they "start again"? Most people's response is, "Not Here!"

II.

Kairos Ministry

KAIROS MEANS "GOD'S special time." The inmates who attend a Kairos experience an outpouring of God's love through the men and women who participate on a team. The inside team through a series of talks remind participants of a God who still loves them, died for them, and offers forgiveness and hope for the future. Isn't that what all of us want?

Women who participate on a Kairos team stay on the outside and prepare home cooked meals, as well as prepare examples of ways in which people are expressing God's love for them. Examples such as letters that each participant receives, a celebration cake, placemats, a prayer chain, etc. The last day, the ladies are allowed to enter the prison and participate in a praise service in which the inmates express what the weekend has meant to them. The only thing they are not allowed to express is "Thanks" because it comes to them through the Love of God, and teams do not take credit for it.

Most of the inmates sign up because they have heard of the home-style meals and cookies. In short, they come to eat! Every Kairos team member contributes 42 dozen cookies since each inmate in the institution is given a dozen cookies, as well as correctional officers. That's somewhere between 2,500 and 4,000 <u>dozen</u> cookies depending on the size of the institution.

This ministry is definitely something you must feel passionate about in order to participate, especially for the women. You ought to try to recruit women to take a weekend off to cook and clean, write 42 letters to men you do not know, bake 42 dozen cookies, and do a variety of other things that need to be done behind the scenes to make the weekend happen. Top that off with entering a prison on Sunday afternoon – which for most women is a "scary" thought. Not the easiest ministry to get people to sign up for! However, once you've been to a closing on Sunday and see the way in which God works in these men's lives in such a short time. It is like watching a miracle occur before your eyes.

There is nothing that will "light the fire" again in a Christian like:

- Being introduced to a man whose eyes were cold as ice and seemed to be full of a dark evil, and watch as his whole demeanor changed and "life" illuminated his eyes.
- Hearing and seeing gang members from different gangs who have expressed only hate for each other standing together with arms draped over each other's shoulders tell a room full of people that they no longer hate each other, that they love each other with the love of Christ. They declare that they are brothers.
- To hear a man who had not received a letter in over 10 years talk about a bag full of letters that he received from people who did not even know him, but they cared enough to share the love of Christ with him.
- To see a man who had never had a birthday cake before break down with tears when he received a celebration cake marking

his new relationship with a God who cared about him, even though he was in prison.

- To experience the hope for a future from a man who is a "toe tagger" (life without the chance of parole) and knows that he will probably never exit the prison system alive.

Overall, the Recidivism Rate (men who leave prison and then return) is over 50%, but the recidivism rate for men who have been through a Kairos is 15%. It is a program that is making a difference. Year after year, we watched as God changed men's lives behind the walls. We even saw some released and begin the process of starting over. We watched as they struggled to find a place to live, an employer that would take a chance and hire a felon, then struggle to simply make ends meet.

III.

An Impression

ABOUT 7 YEARS ago, Clayton, was going out of town on business. He had just finished teaching a Sunday school class to youth, grabbed a bite to eat, and was headed down the road in his suburban to an appointment later that evening. As he approached an intersection he noticed a pickup that had stopped and seemed to be waiting for Clayton to pass on by. However, after stopping at the stop sign, the man starting pulling out and he T-boned Clayton. He just had not seen Clayton; he saw the vehicle behind Clayton and thought he had plenty of time. Once he hit Clayton's suburban, it went airborne and flipped, landing on its roof as it skidded down the highway. Clayton remembers the glass from the front windshield shattering as the roof started caving in, and then the momentum rolled the car on its side and it rolled three or four times, landing on its side. Clayton tried to gather himself together once the SUV had stopped rolling, and he thinks that he must have passed out for a short period of time. When he came to he smelled battery acid and decided it was time to climb out of driver side door which was above him.

As he started to climb out one of the young ladies he had taught earlier that morning screamed, "He's alive". Apparently, a small group had come up on the accident and thought that the person inside was dead. They had called 911 and the police and a fire truck with the EMT's arrived within just a few minutes after the call. The violence of the crash was very apparent the next day when we went to look at the suburban, it looked more like a corvette. The passenger side roof was below the dashboard, and it was clear that the only place a person could have survived the crash was where Clayton was sitting.

When we left the place where the vehicle had been towed, we were both in agreement with what the newscasters had declared was a walking miracle. Clayton had walked away from a vehicle that had flipped once and rolled three more times with only a very sore body and a concussion. As we read the paper over the next few months, we were stunned by the number of people that died after having only rolled once. We knew that God wasn't through with Clayton yet! The wreck made him really start to look closely at his life. It kind of changed our perspective because we both knew how quickly the outcome could have been different. We were convinced that Clayton had been spared for a reason.

One morning a short time after the wreck, I was standing in the kitchen when Clayton said that he felt like God was putting something on his heart, that he was supposed to do more than just preach once a month out at the prison and do a couple of Kairos a year. He felt like he should be helping some of these men whose lives had changed as a result of asking Jesus into their lives.

He talked about how he had watched them struggle and felt like they ran up against one obstacle after another. He felt that if he got a house and rented it out to 2 or 3 men that they could share the costs, and make it an affordable situation until they could get on their feet. He asked me what I thought. I told him that he better do whatever God told him; he should not think that when he died and went to heaven and God asked him why he didn't do what God asked of him that it wasn't going to get him off the hook to say, "Well I wanted to do it but Connie didn't want me too". That wasn't going to cut it!

We envisioned simply helping 2 or 3 men, and doing our part. We started small, got a rent house and fixed it up, but the neighborhood was not happy. In fact, they revolted. It was Halloween, and they called the TV station, and posted signs at the end of the block saying that perverts lived at _____ address. The men were scared and did not stay the night at the house. The house was egged, and the TV station showed only a snippet of the interview with Clayton in which he tried to explain the ministry. It became very apparent that we had to do something else.

We started looking for a place outside the city limits, in the county. We found a couple of places that we felt would work, but each time as it came to close the deal, the deal fell through.

Then Clayton told me about a friend who was interested in selling his place. It was an old trailer with pull outs, and twenty years earlier he had built a nice frame for a garage/workshop, house, and decking. It was just that his wife had divorced him, and he never finished it. Here was 40 acres of land, with an unfinished frame already up, and it was filled with clothes, tapes, memories, junk from twenty years and lots of cats who had especially liked the carpet. When Clayton told me the price I looked at him like he was crazy and told him we were not paying that much money for this.

We kept looking and nothing worked out. One morning as I was driving to work, a thought popped into my mind "What if I was the reason that Clayton was not able to start the ministry?" I immediately called Clayton and said, "Honey, I want you to call Jim Mauldin and tell him to meet us at Texas Burger at 11:30 and then we will go out and look at his place again. Maybe, you can draw up for me what you see as far as the house goes, and how to make it work." Clayton was silent for a minute and then said, "Oh, that's weird." About 10 minutes earlier he had called Jim Mauldin and told him to meet us at Texas Burger at 11:30 and we would go out and look at the place again. I knew when we went out there that God had picked this place -- what I saw or did not see was irrelevant.

Clayton drew a diagram of what he envisioned to be possible with the frame and the land and the adventure began. I must credit Jim Mauldin for having a tremendous amount of faith. The financial arrangements (owner financed with no payment due until 6 months after the contract was signed) were not exactly what a seller wants to hear, but Jim shared both the vision and passion for helping formerly incarcerated men, as he also works the Kairos Ministry. So, God provided the place.

The next part was to start to clean up and refurbish the trailer, making it habitable for a few men and then starting to finish out the existing frame with sheetrock, plumbing, electrical, installing heating/air conditioning, and painting – all with personal investment & contributions from people that God provided at just the right time. We found the saying "God is never late, and never early. He's always on time" to be true! When it seemed as though there wasn't enough money, God always provided it. The time that immediately comes to mind is when we did not have air conditioning which is a must in Midland, TX., with 100+ degree temperatures in the summers. A check showed up in the mail for the exact amount. Along the way a friend bought carpet, people donated their furniture to us as they bought new pieces for their homes.

All the while, Clayton continued working at the bank. About 2 years into the project He was stressed to the max. His job at the bank, and Stepping Stone Ministry (which had grown to 17 men) were both full time jobs and too much for one man to handle. Clayton ended up walking away from the job of trust manager for real estate at the bank (an income of $60,000 a year) to full time director of Stepping Stone Ministry. The first year he earned a total of $12,000.

IV.

Stepping Stone

STEPPING STONE HAS been in existence approximately 6 years now. It is amazing to see the current facility that the Lord has built, a ranch style house that will hold up to 50 men. It currently houses between 45 and 50 men who are in the process of starting over and adjusting to the "free world." There is an application process that they must go through in order to be approved to be accepted as a resident. Since Stepping Stone is a private half-way house, we do not take any money from the state or the federal government because we do not want them telling us who we must take. The whole premise is built on our belief that Christ can make a new creation out of a person. We want to be sure that the men we accept are serious about changing their lives, and making their personal relationship with Christ the guiding force in their new life.

When they first come out of prison they are given a bus ticket to where they are going and $50. Ask yourself, what kind of start in life is $50 and a bus ticket? The $50 does not go very far; you can choose to eat or find a cheap motel for a night. When they arrive they are picked up at the bus station by Clayton or a member of Stepping Stone. Usually this occurs at somewhere between 1 and 2 o'clock in the morning. The next morning one of their first orders of business is to report to the parole office, and then they start the process of getting an ID or Driver's License, Social Security Card, etc. At Stepping Stone, Clayton tells them that the first two weeks their job is to find a job. This is part of their learning to accept responsibility and to become accountable. After obtaining a job, they are expected to pay $450 for rent and contribute

$200 for food per month. If they are on a monitor they pay $50 a month for it. They have agreed to stay for a minimum of 4 months, and they can stay a maximum of 1 year. When they apply they sign a Resident's Agreement which outlines the amounts of money and the rules they agree to abide by. We view this as giving their word, and expect them to act with integrity. When a man first reaches Stepping Stone he is provided with sheets, towels, personal toiletries, and clothes. It quickly adds up to somewhere around $400 per individual. If they leave before the 4 months are up it becomes very hard to recoup the initial investment in the man which makes it difficult to keep providing the necessities as new men continue to arrive.

Part of the program is that they also are expected to attend at least 2 Bible Studies per week, attend at least 1 church service, and complete 2 hours of community service hours per week, either at the house or for some service organization that needs it. Since we are 1 of approximately 6 houses in the State of Texas that accepts sexual offenders we also provide a worship service on Sunday mornings for the men who cannot participate in a service where playground equipment is on site or be within a certain distance from a park or school area. Also, Bible studies are conducted 4 nights onsite at Stepping Stone.

Men also are placed in teams to keep the house clean, cook evening meals, and perform basic chores which serve to develop a pride in their home. Duties are rotated every month. They learn to clean up after themselves and take care of business. They are encouraged that this is their home and they need to care for it and they are encouraged to become a family. Stepping Stone's name is descriptive of being the first step on their journey into the Christian community and into society. Stepping Stone treats them as men, and they are expected to act like Christ followers. We have found that men have come in to our lives for a time, and then they get their foundations set and they move on. However, they don't move out. They have walked into our lives, and found a place in our hearts. Some of the sweetest memories are things like a surprise birthday party for Clayton thrown a month after his birthday, just so they could surprise him! Since Clayton is a "die hard

Texas Aggie" the decorations & attire chosen for the party was Texas Orange, Red Raider Black & Red, etc.

Then there are men who find ways to begin their own ministry, such as Ron Mitchell who told me when he first arrived at Stepping Stone that he was called to a ministry of encouragement. He began a ministry of texting a scripture everyday and a positive thought that went with it. At last count he sends out over 250 positive messages a day. He works at a funeral home and is a man who walks out his faith. The compassion and personal empathy he gives to the clients makes a lasting impression on them, as well as the men who he mentors when they first come out of prison. He has become one of Stepping Stone's team captains, and is the kind of man that we want as role models and mentors at Stepping Stone. He has walked in their shoes on the inside, and he is walking in Christ's footsteps outside.

I know that Stepping Stone is making a difference when men like Robert come up and share with me their stories. Robert is a quiet, humble man, who comes across as rather shy. One afternoon he came in looking for Clayton, with a big smile and he seemed to be bursting with excitement. The company he works for had just had a luncheon and had started an award that is to be given to the most outstanding employee for the year. He had been working for them about 9 months and had been selected as the award winner! He was beaming. He told me that there were men who had been working there several years so it never even crossed his mind that he would get the award. He was overwhelmed and overjoyed. Isn't it nice when someone recognizes your accomplishments and tells you so?

Last Christmas was a memorable one. Many of the men got into the Christmas spirit and wanted to decorate the house. We ended up with several Christmas trees; two in the main house and one in the addition (Chapel area), and one in the mobile home which can house up to 9 men. It really hit me hard when one of the team captains and I were talking, and he shared with me that one of the men over 40 years in age said, as he was decorating the tree, "I can't believe this. My parents never did anything like this. This is the first Christmas tree I've ever had." It really made me stop and think about how blessed I had been to have Christian parents who introduced me to Christ early and explain to me that "He" is the reason for the season.

When we first started holding Sunday services at Stepping Stone for the men who could not attend elsewhere, we started with 5 or 6 men. Now, we are having anywhere from 20-25 every Sunday because that is where they want to be. We have a group of men and women out of the small town of Greenwood, TX. who come on the 3rd Sunday of every month that play guitars, lead us in great music, and speak from their heart when they bring the message. Clayton usually brings 2 services out of the month, and then has guest preachers/teachers the other 2 services. As I write this, Easter was yesterday, and we had a sweet service. For the special music, one of the residents blessed us by signing (sign language) the song, "He's Alive". God has sent men who are tremendously talented musically, as well as a man who makes custom wooden crosses, plaques, clocks. They are men whose hearts have been changed by the love of Christ.

V.

People of Principle (Pop)

TO FULLY APPRECIATE God's guidance one must know that even before Clayton left the bank, the Lord was preparing both of us for the new paths He had lined out for our journey. In the months before Clayton went full time at Stepping Stone he kept reminding me that a friend of ours had just received a Federal grant on Fatherhood and he needed a Project Manager. He said that I should apply for that position. After teaching/coaching for 35 years I had retired and had begun a second career in real estate. I had just finished up a couple of specialty credentials and was excited about pursing that path. Of course I had no idea that the housing market was about to face a reversal nationwide, and even though Midland was not affected as drastically as other cities, the impact was felt.

I applied to People of Principle in November of 2007, and basically did not hear anything until January 2008. At that time, I agreed to go help in setting up the office and start working with the Educational Director, Ron Brewer. Did I mention that this grant involved going into prisons in West Texas and taking an educational seminar on Healthy Marriages? Once again, I believe that God laughs.

The grant that Tim Baum, (Executive Director) had received was in the Fatherhood area, but the grant POP was awarded specifically involved marriage education to improve the couples marriages. Statistics show that within the first year of an inmate's release 85% of those couples divorce. Most of the prison Chaplains and Wardens had been in favor of an educational program dealing with fatherhood, since many of the inmates were fathers. That was an easy sell; however, when we first approached the program coordinators (Chaplains) on the idea of conducting a marriage seminar inside the prison with the inmate's wives in attendance, sitting next to them in a prison, it was quite a different response. One of the Chaplains answer was "No", unequivocally no. There was no way on earth that we were going to bring women into his prison, end of story. This seemed to be the response of most of the units, until a new Chaplain arrived at one of the units, and shared with Ron that you have to know what you are promoting, and how to promote it. The first thing you must stress is safety and security. Then you have to let the Chaplains know that they can satisfy all of their family requirements for the year in this one weekend. Then you must reassure them of your commitment to safety and security. That one, brave chaplain, gave us the opportunity to enter the unit and successfully conduct the first POP (People of Principle) seminar.

After the first seminar was successful, and the Chaplain shared with other Chaplains in his region that he believed it had a positive impact on the men in his unit, we were up and running. The first Chaplain who had told us "unequivocally no", later called Ron and asked if we would come to his unit, and he also became one of our strongest advocates.

People of Principle (POP) was a name that our organization took seriously. We wanted to manage the federal funding in such a way as to bring honor and glory to the Lord – to be above reproach and to honor all federal expectations. We looked at the federal grant as a gift from

God which gave us the opportunity to help couples in dire straits. As such, we worked very hard to abide by the federal government rules, and to do things the way the federal system wanted it done. During the government portion of the program we offered educational information, and different tools for improving communication and their marriages. It was our goal as believers to let the couples see that there was something different about us. Once we closed out the federal government portion of the grant we could share with them what we believed gave them the power to make those tools work - Christ in the center of their lives and marriage. It was our desire that they would come to recognize the difference on Sunday was our relationship with Jesus. We don't believe that you have to beat people over the head with a Bible, but we wanted them to see us living the walk, not just talking it.

The last four years have been one of the most fulfilling experiences of my life. Clayton and I spent at least one and usually two weekends out of the month entering prisons and conducting marriage seminars. Sometimes, we had teams in multiple units. One of the most unique aspects of our seminars was that we had several teachers who were ex-offenders. Those were the teachers that the couples listened most intently too. They knew that these couples had walked in their shoes, and they had made it. They offered hope to the incarcerated couples. Over the course of five years we served 607 couples, which is amazing since it took us over a year to get into the prison system.

The marriage seminar presented a variety of modules which dealt with nationwide marriage statistics as well as incarceration specific stats. The seminar then went on to talk about choices – good and bad choices, the reduced number of choices an incarcerated person was allowed to make. Did you know that as a free world person we make approximately 2,500 choices a day? When a person becomes incarcerated that number drops to around 250 choices a day. We presented tools to improve communication, units on anger management, domestic violence, recognizing your partner's love language, and the module which became the focal point of the seminar "The Institutionalized Mind."

POP also learned to be flexible. There was a substantial amount of prep work that had to occur before a seminar could be taken into a unit. We had a cadre of approximately 40 teachers, all of which had to be trained as a TDJC Volunteer and as a POP presenter. We had to make contact with the chaplains and see if they were interested in having the program and set up a meeting to make a presentation to the Chaplain and Warden. If you are considering entering a prison with some type of ministry it is very important that you already have an established relationship with the warden or the Chaplain who often serves as the program coordinator for the unit, or you need to cultivate such a relationship. They need to know that you are trustworthy, dependable, and aware of the necessity of abiding by the rules and regulations of the system. If they agreed to have the marriage seminar in their unit then we began the process of working with the Chaplain to announce the program, have the inmate fill out an application, and send it to his wife. The wife then would fill in her information and mail it back to the Chaplain who would then start to do the background check on the wives, and the inmates. The inmates could not have had a major case in the last few months. This really served to be a positive influence on discipline in the prisons since in order to come to a Follow-Up Session the inmate had to keep his discipline record clear. Again, this information was tracked by the Chaplain. This amounted to a lot of extra time put in by the Chaplains on a unit which was over and above their regular job. Once the Chaplain had approved the list of participants he then sent POP a list of the wives names, addresses, and phone numbers so we could contact the wives and let them know the dates for the weekend of the seminar, and they could start to make arrangements to get off from their jobs, and make childcare arrangements. POP then started making the arrangements for motel accommodations, transportation arrangements, POP teachers, and to verify as best as we could that the ladies were coming. Making contact with the wives would usually take several days because they were screening calls for bill collectors and they were very hesitant to verify their identity. Once we explained that we were the marriage seminar that went into the prisons and that we didn't want anything from them we could start to build a relationship.

POP learned to be extremely flexible because you would enter one unit and they would do things a certain way, but the next unit you went into the following week would do things a little differently. You had to be patient, kind, organized and keep a smile on your face all the time. We found out at our first seminar that all paper materials had to be printed in black and white only; we were later told any colored ink could be turned into an ink to be used in making tattoos. When equipment such as sound systems, movie mates, projector screens, were taken into the units, all were inspected, and all must be listed on a previously sent inventory list. Pens & pencils had to be counted before and the same number must be accounted for after use.

Some tidbits you may find interesting if considering starting a prison ministry: Computers are not allowed in Texas prisons due to unsupervised communication problems, so we were allowed to make DVD Discs of each module of the program and play them on a movie mate projector.

Clear, see through containers must be used to transport various items. Food for the meals we brought in were packaged in a see through bag or plastic container. Beans were often put in a zip-lock baggie so that an officer could squeeze the bag and feel if there was contraband present. No sugar was allowed in due to the fact that it could be used to make alcohol. So, sweeteners such as splenda, sweet & low were put into baggies and marked as to their brand.

Teachers and the ladies entering the prison are told to wear modest clothing, close toed shoes, and colored shirts and pants. Inmates are all dressed in white and the officers in gray. If something was to happen such as a riot, the people in the bright colored clothing would be easy to spot.

It is a felony for anyone to take a cell phone into a prison. There are so many reasons for cell phones to be banned inside, one of which is the fact that death threats and hits have been ordered on people simply by gaining access to a cell phone. Simple items we take for granted can be used for evil. For this reason we told the ladies who were participating in a POP seminar that the only thing which they were to take in or out was their picture ID.

At any time a prison can be put on lockdown. That means that all of the preparations that were made, and the ladies & teachers could show up at the prison that morning, and we would have to cancel the seminar if the prison had been locked down. The way POP felt is that we were guests in the Warden's house, and we appreciated all of the safeguards and security they could provide, and I must say that the authorities did an excellent job.

I will never forget the first group of ladies that came to our very first seminar. Ron Brewer and I were putting together a little green cart which we were going to use to take in the equipment the next morning. Three ladies who had driven about five hours from the Ft. Worth area arrived at Believer's Fellowship in Ft. Stockton where we were to have our first pre-seminar meeting. We were going to take Friday evening to meet the ladies, go over the rules & regulations for going into the unit, and grab a bite to eat together to start to get to know them. However, their honesty about not even being sure that they wanted to attend the seminar made us stop and listen. One of them said, "Look, if all you are going to do is tell us that we should stay married to them and when they get out we have to simply hand over the check book and car keys while they go off with their homeboys and do what they did to get thrown into prison, then I want you to know that I don't need to be here. I want a divorce."

With that conversation the grant began to change, as we began to listen and realize that while the men inside had programs available for education, drug & alcohol abuse programs, three meals and a place to sleep each night, their wives did not. Their wives had been left to shoulder the load, to be both father & mother, to handle all of the responsibility from providing shelter, clothing, and food to being the disciplinarian. For most ladies it involved working two jobs just to keep a roof over their head, then going home to cook supper, help with homework, get everyone ready for bed, start to write him a letter only to find herself falling asleep as she wrote it. Knowing that he would be angry because she didn't write him and that tomorrow morning she would simply start the process all over again. When she could finally save enough money to drive five hours to go see him, he would be ticked off that she had not written him enough, and once again the visit would either start off or soon turn sour as she was supposed to explain why the letters were not written daily, or why she had not put more money on his books, and he wanted to be filled in on everything that had happened since the last visit. It was becoming clear to POP staff that while she had grown in maturity, was taking responsibility for the family, providing shelter and clothing for herself and the children; in short had learned that she could make it without him. She was not going to put up with the same old behaviors, she didn't have to. There was just one hiccup, she still loved him. She wanted to believe they could still make it.

VI.

Silent Cries

For just a moment try to put yourself into each of these situations:

- Imagine that as you turn onto your street at the end of it there are police car lights, flashing bright red & blue. Immediately you are gripped with fear, something's wrong, one of the kids must be hurt, has my husband had a heart attack? Your mind races as you pull into the driveway and get out of the car. As the policeman approaches you know that your life has been changed forever – you just don't know how. . . .

- Another scenario involves you talking quietly, confidentially with a co-worker that you perceive is a new friend. She seems so nice, has made you actually hurt as you laugh at her humor. It has been so long since you had a friend you could trust, maybe you could actually share your well-kept secret, but the next day as you walk into the office for a cup of coffee - you know. Everyone stops talking and turns to stare. It's a look of pity and distrust . . . They know. She told them . . .

- Or possibly, you have rushed to the school to pick up your child. As you pull the car against the curb, she runs toward you with a look of pain. The other kids are taunting her. Through a mere slip of the tongue she told the class that her daddy doesn't live at home, he's in prison. . . .

-

These stories play out every day in the lives of some of the women I have had the pleasure to meet the past few years. I must tell you straight up that before I became Project Manager for a grant that takes healthy marriage seminars into prisons, I had no idea of the struggles these ladies encounter every single day. In fact, my opinion was that anyone who was married to a man in prison must be "white trash", or <u>crazy!</u>

To say that my opinion has changed over the last four years would be a huge understatement. What I found were women who were from all "walks of life" struggling simply to survive. They are professional ladies, business managers, church secretaries, part time students with little education, full time students working two jobs who are in a hurry to get an education! They have found that they simply cannot provide the basics for their children, so they do double and triple duty in order to be able to get a job that will enable them to earn more. These ladies have earned both my respect and admiration.

The most interesting part of what I have learned is that you may work in the next cubicle or live next door to these ladies and you will most likely never know of their struggle - because of the stigma attached to their situation. They simply have learned not to tell anyone. Usually, they have learned that the hard way. In America, we will mount fundraisers, take up collections, and establish bank accounts for people who have had tragedies wipe out all their earthly possessions. We are a nation who sends money overseas to help starving children in other countries, all of which are excellent causes; however, we are not as inclined to want to help some felon's kid. After all, as I have been told, they are in prison for a reason. They deserve to be there. I must say that I agree. I am not the volunteer who wants to throw open the doors and release them all. Maybe you are like me and did not really realize that the children and the spouses are "serving time" right along with the inmate. The difference is that they are paying for crimes that they did not commit.

Did you know that children of incarcerated parents are 6 times more likely to be incarcerated and 11 times more likely to engage in violent behavior? We don't really want to think about that. But in truth, do you want your child sitting next to that kid in class whose father is in prison? Do you really want to know about that lady two cubicles down which it is rumored has a husband in prison? "Heavens No" that kid might be a bad influence on my child, or she would probably just be asking for money all the time.

If we are honest that is the way we think about it; if we think about it at all. Now we would not verbalize it, but it is the way most middle-class people feel. Other reasons include:

1. What will people think if they see me with her?
2. Her son might teach my son bad habits, there's no telling what he learns at home.
3. If I become her friend and he gets out we could unwittingly be drawn into their world of violence, he might send someone to hurt my family.
4. They probably use drugs and would try selling it to my kids. They might get my kids hooked on drugs.
5. They are just not the type of people we want to associate with.

You see, it's just not a socially acceptable situation that they are in. We want to help, but not personally. We are actually afraid of them, especially the sex offenders. Do you realize that you could be living next door to an axe murderer and never know it, but if you live next door to a sex offender you will be sent notification? He must register the rest of his life. (I really don't have a problem with the notification, but let's apply it to all major crimes, such as murder, drug trafficking, etc.) Through my husband's experience with running Stepping Stone, a private halfway house, we have found that the success rate for starting a new life is a lot higher for sex offenders than druggies or alcohol addicts. Once a man gets a few dollars ahead and he has the means to buy alcohol he falls for the old line of just one drink won't hurt, or I'll just do one line of cocaine, ecstasy, whatever your drug of choice is; however, as the ladies who live with these men know too well. One line turns into two, one beer with the guys turns into several, and . . . the tumblers start to turn, and the door starts to swing open for them to head back. Ironically, each one truly believes that it won't be him. Statistics show that 90% were on drugs or alcohol when they committed the offense that got them locked up. Unfortunately, the statistics on recidivism are sobering as well. The national average in America is that over 50% of men who are released from prison end up back inside within 3 years.

VI.

Institutionalized Mind

ONE OF THE unique modules POP presented inside was a curriculum that Ron Brewer (Educational Director of POP) developed called "The Institutionalized Mind". The module was the focal point of the weekend seminars we conducted. Ron has been involved with the prison system for over 18 years in a variety of ways. He has worked in the Wyndham School System, volunteered in prison ministry, served on the board of the non-profit Stepping Stone Ministry and as Educational Director of POP.

This module promoted understanding between the couple of the challenges that each faces in the unique circumstances that incarceration and re-entry brings. It presented some of the survival tools that most men develop when incarcerated such as: self-centeredness, intimidation, and manipulation. The interesting thing to watch in this module was how many of the men would tell their wives "yes this is true, but it does not affect me".

Ron would often ask the men "Who looks out for you in here?" To which the response would be "No one. I watch out for myself." They had to. It was natural to develop a heightened sense of self-centered behavior. Intimidation had to be portrayed in order to not be seen as weak and to become a target. Manipulation was a game they played to see if they could get something from someone who did not want to give it to them. They especially like to manipulate volunteers and see if they can hold something over them and threaten to get them in trouble. They try to get volunteers to take a note to someone for them, or a letter, which are violations. The volunteer who falls for it may be carrying out information for a gang or even a hit on someone and not even realize it.

While these are survival tools inside – if they continue these behaviors it will surely destroy their marriages on the outside. Possibly a reason for the 85% divorce rate within the first year of release. One lady just blurted out "Ron, why didn't you tell me this 20 years ago. I just thought that he didn't love me." She had remarried the same man who had been sent back to prison.

We wondered if women who had been incarcerated developed the same habits or tools for survival. At one of our seminars the wife of one of the inmates had also been incarcerated. She talked at length with Ron assuring him that the information applied to the women as well. She shared that her daughter shortly after she had come home had asked her, "Mommy, why don't you love me anymore?" She replied, "Silly, I do love you. Why would you ask that?" Her daughter said, "You don't hold me anymore." She told Ron that she sat and wept as she realized that she didn't pick her child up and hold her. She said that she always kept a distance between her and another person. It was a defense mechanism, and she had not even realized it, until her daughter asked the question.

The Institutionalized Mind was the module that ended with a question and answer session. It was usually taught by an ex-offender, and then his wife would join him and talk about the incarceration and release from her perspective. Actually, we learned more from this module about the specifics of incarceration and how it affects marriages but also the family as well. It was a time of feedback in which the couples began to piece together how the changes in their lives had affected them as individuals, couples and their children. For many of the men their children remained in their minds just as when they had left for prison. When in reality the child had grown into a teenager or young adult.

POP had so many concerns about the children of these families and how they were being affected. We brought in a lady by the name of Marilyn Gambrell, founder of No More Victims, Inc., (non-profit), an advocacy agency for newborns and children of incarcerated parents, to train us and make us better informed and prepared in this area. Marilyn's program is based in Houston, TX, where she works with children experiencing the trauma of one or both parents being currently incarcerated or parents who have been released from incarceration. She began her career as a parole officer and after witnessing the pain that so many of the children were experiencing as a direct result of parental incarceration, she left parole to begin working with children of incarcerated parents within the school system to provide emotional, physical and academic support. She believed that this is where she needed to be to reach the most children and to have the greatest impact. There was a Lifetime Movie made about her life: "Fighting the Odds-The Marilyn Gambrell Story". Jamie Gertz played Ms. Gambrell's character in the movie.

When Ron Brewer first approached Marilyn about helping POP in reuniting children with their incarcerated parents her response brought about a new awareness for him. It was not what he expected. Marilyn shared with him that there were many other variables to be considered when embarking on this mission to reunite incarcerated parents and formerly incarcerated parents with their children. "You have to consider what have the experiences of the children been with this parent prior to their incarceration and during their incarceration?" stated Ms. Gambrell. "There is often tremendous anger, hurt, abuse, feelings of rejection and many other feelings that the incarcerated parent needs to be aware of as possibilities and how to cope with those potential feelings and potential responses from the child toward the incarcerated parent. It wasn't until later that we realized what she meant. Marilyn had seen so many tragedies that fell on the children because of their parent's behavior. She brought a whole new perspective to the problem.

When she came to do the training for POP she presented at some of the prisons in our area as well. She brought with her 2 young members of the No More Victims Family and Mr. Ivory Mayhorn. The presentation they made at the prison was a reality check. Through a role play involving a volunteer from the inmates, they staged a scenario of the inmate seeing his child for the first time since he was released. It involved a set of circumstances which often occurs where the inmate and the child stop writing and communicating over the years and in most cases, there never was any communication. The father seeks out the child after release. We had not considered the amount of anger, and hurt the child had stored up. When the two young No More Victims Family members, one female and one male, portrayed the situation, they brought hard hitting, eye opening reality to the reenactment. In fact, I sat there holding my breath thinking, "Oh no, we are going to have a problem here." The inmate bowed up and gave the natural response of "You don't talk to me like that, I'm your father." To which the young female responded, "You're not my father, you haven't been there for my birthdays, you never walked me to school, I haven't seen nor heard from you in 16 years. I don't know you." The inmate stepped back, looked to Marilyn and shook his head – he didn't know what to do. As we all learned that day the children have years of anger and bitterness that they have kept locked inside, and the reaction returning incarcerated fathers receive is often not what they expected. Then we found out why.

Each of the two young No More Victims family members gave their stories to the audience, and you knew immediately why they felt the way they did. Their stories were horrific - one's mother had tried to poison her. Then Marilyn got up and explained what she sees and works with on a daily basis. She first hand witnesses the overwhelming violence, hurt, and death that has been thrust on the greater majority of children that she works with and how they have no one to help them. That is where Marilyn comes in. She "stands in the gap" as their parent figure. She builds a trust with them, and works to make them realize that they can do something different with their lives. She encourages them to get an education and that the cycle of crime, violence and incarceration within their family that they have been born into… stops with them. She helps them to believe in themselves because they have been told that they are worthless and they will end up in prison just like their mother and/or father, and will never make something of themselves. Marilyn's kids call her "Mama". Her program is both successful and incredible. The children in her program are graduating from high school and now college….and they are not going to the penitentiary. The love that Marilyn has for her children and the love they have for her is amazing.

After Marilyn's training, we realized that there is so much more that needs to be done to prepare these incarcerated fathers for the day that they are released and return to society, and hopefully, their families. Once again we realized that there needed to be programs available for the women and children.

In the POP Marriage seminars we had noticed that as we ended the module "The Institutionalized Mind" the mood was often quiet and sober, as the discussion centered upon the habits he had developed for survival, (self-centeredness, intimidation, and manipulation). Slowly, the couples were beginning to recognize that there was a conflict waiting to happen due to the way that the wives had matured and assumed more responsibility, had learned to provide for the family, handle the money, pay the bills, stick to an impossibly small budget, and juggle a million tasks at once. All while he had become stuck in a time warp that did not allow him to make decisions, or prepare him for the world he would reenter after years of confinement with a label attached that would forever hinder his opportunities to obtain employment. The lost time with his children and wife that could never be regained. The reality that when he is released the worst is not over, but the battle is just beginning. The sense of the reality and hopelessness is sobering and there seemed to be a heaviness that settled over the couples.

VII.

Texas Arms of Love

I HAVE SHARED THAT this grant was a federal grant, and as such there were certain modules we were required to cover, certain things we were allowed to do and certain things we were not allowed to do in the federal portion of the program. After we had delivered between 8-12 hours of instruction, we were allowed to close out the federal portion of the grant and offer for the participants to stay for a faith based portion of the program which came under the umbrella of a non-profit known as "Texas Arms of Love".

Texas Arms of Love is a non-profit run by a man of great faith, Steve Becker. He is a man that I have learned much from. His humbleness does not even allow him to acknowledge how many entities operate under him. When asked, he simply laughs, and says, "I don't know. I quit counting." To Steve all that matters is that Christ is glorified.

After POP closed out the federal portion of the grant, we would start the faith based part of the program. We usually started with several minutes of praise & worship songs. Sometimes we sang to a

DVD or sometimes there were team members who played instruments and it was live. What always amazed us were the numerous couples that shared that this was the first time that they had ever worshiped together. That had been something that had not been a priority in their lives. We even had a couple that were atheists who stayed. We did not know at the time that they were atheists. After the seminar was complete the wife shared that she had really enjoyed the movie. We had permission from "Fireproof" to show the movie inside of prisons. Since the movie was about a couple who was struggling and considering divorce, complete with all of the stresses of today's lifestyle it was definitely a story that couples could identify with. We also felt that the movie did a great job of laying out the plan of salvation as well as presenting the hope that a personal relationship with Jesus offers. The wife wrote Ron about 2 weeks later sharing that she had started looking for a church to attend, and that her husband had started going to the services inside the prison.

If you visited with the POP teachers and staff you would find that we believe that the importance of faith and hope being offered through the relationship with Christ in the center of their marriage really becomes the turning point in the whole program. That might not be what the Feds want to hear, but the reality of faith is what gives the couples hope for the future, not just tools of education. Truly, Christ is the power behind the tools which causes them to work. He is the hope that they are looking for.

I believe that God used the seminars to change not only the participants but the teachers as well. In 2010, People of Principle was honored to have been chosen as one of the presenters at the Annual Conference in Washington, D.C. We were able to take along one of our teaching couples. Formerly incarcerated; Billy is now a vice president of an oil company. He and his wife LaMarque have a very inspiring story to share about overcoming. While they were in Washington, Billy & LaMarque were able to serve on a Fatherhood panel. Billy passionately shared about the difficulties and the special moments of blessing of becoming a step-father. He addressed the difficulties associated with discipline, love, and acceptance between the child and the step-father. The importance of a Fatherhood Program especially to incarcerated men is a topic Billy believes strongly in. He believes that the need in such programs is great in order to break the cycle of incarceration. Everyone left that session filled with hope that if this couple could make it, others could also.

At one of the seminars the first year I was sitting next to a young couple that was so cute. He started sharing with me about his family and mentioned that he had triplets for sisters. One sister was a church secretary, one sister was married to a preacher, and one sister and her husband had just recently returned from China where they had been teacher/missionaries. As I sat there listening, the question that popped into my mind was "How did you end up in prison?" It was obvious that he had been raised well. Then almost as if knowing what I was thinking he started sharing about how he had become involved with drugs, and how quickly his life had changed. Sometime, in the midst of listening, I realized that this could be my son. In fact, it could be almost anyone's child. The difference was that he got caught. All of our children at different times in their lives make poor choices. As parents, we can try to teach them about the dangers of sex, drugs, and alcohol --- but we are not the ones who make the choice. Sometime during that conversation the couple had ceased to be a number/name and became real people to me.

One of our Teacher Couples, Barbara & Oscar, liked to do something very special at the beginning of each seminar. They gave each woman a rose to begin the seminar. These roses were given from their hearts to the ladies to let them know how special and beautiful they are. They would tell the ladies that the rose was a gift that their husband wanted to give to the wife. Barbara and Oscar had walked in the shoes of these couples and have a special love for them.

Throughout the five years that POP existed we found that there is a big difference between seeing a name of a wife on paper or the number of the incarcerated man, and meeting that individual in person. As God allowed us to see the person our perspectives changed. We actually got to see them through His eyes, with His heart. We found that for a few hours we got to be the "hands and feet" of Christ reaching out in compassion, which is what we as believers are supposed to do daily. It was getting out of the pew, and walking out of the physical walls of a church building and into a person's life to offer that hope that Christ will meet them at their point of need.

VIII.

Couples We Have Met

OVER THE COURSE of the last four years of the grant we have often talked of the many humorous situations we had experienced. Our office was definitely not the "norm". Our staff was all very hands on and involved in all aspects of the program. Friday mornings we would spend loading up for seminars. One particular day it turned out that some of the local churches were going to have a prayer time & protest the abortion issue at the Planned Parenthood facility. Planned Parenthood just happened to be next door to the building where we officed. This particular day we were late in getting loaded up, so we were trying to load the trailer with all of our heavy equipment, using dollies. One of the dollies got loose and rolled out the door, over my foot, and into the street with me chasing, hopping on one foot, and yelling at the top of my lungs. Ron and Mindi were bent over laughing at the whole situation because they noticed that the protestors all paused in their prayers and looked to see what was going on. I had disrupted the prayer service.

Along the way we had some amazing experiences, some humorous and some brought sadness. For the purposes of this book in order to protect their privacy and trust in POP, the stories will be shared with the names of couples and persons that we worked with changed or omitted.

One of the funniest stories came from a wife who was traveling several hours in order to make the seminar. She and her sons had left after she had completed her shift about 10 pm. Her oldest son had just obtained his driver's license, and was going to take the first few hours of driving while she slept. He started out pretty well and drove for a couple of hours. Then she heard her son say "Oh, mama, they are going to take us to jail!" Flashing red and blue lights were right behind their car. Her son was scared, and she kept instructing him to pull over and stop. He did so, and the policeman approached the car with his flashlight. He told the young man that he had stopped him because he seemed to be weaving. When he realized that the young man was a new driver, he just told him to hold the car between the lines. Since the mother was now wide awake she went ahead and took over and started driving. She had been driving for about an hour when she hit a javalina (wild pig) – only in West Texas. The noise was loud as it thudded against the undercarriage. Both boys were instantly awake! Thankfully, the car was not damaged and still drivable so she pulled back onto the road and started off, when there was a whisper of a voice from the younger son. "Mom, I need for you to stop, that scared me so bad that I have to use the bathroom, right now!" She pulled over, and the young man dropped his drawers. He was so focused on business that he did not notice that Mom had slowly inched the car forward a little bit at a time. As Mom and older brother laughed hysterically, he started to run towards the vehicle. He hopped into the backseat, and started yelling, "Ow! Ow! Ow!" It seems like when he dropped his drawers they fell into a patch of stickers! They had no problem staying awake as they drove the rest of the way to the seminar!

Couple 1. It was pretty obvious from the kiss of greeting, as well as the closed body language and unspoken communication of icicles that seemed to be frozen in midair that this couple had major problems. There were no "stolen kisses" or even an indication that either of them desired to kiss the other, kind of strange for a marriage seminar. On

Sunday morning we found the reason why. Ron began talking to the young man and generally asked him what he had thought of the seminar so far. When the young man told Ron that before he answered the question Ron had to understand that he and his wife had really attended the seminar just so that they could have time to plan out their divorce. They had to decide where to put all the children from each of their previous relationships as well as their relationship – sort of a yours, mine, and ours family. The young man told Ron that when he had gone back to his cell last night his "cellie" (cellmate) had asked him if he had enjoyed the seminar. He told him "no". You know how I've told you that she is the one with the problems. They did this module and I found out that I'm the one with the problems. It hasn't been her at all, it's me. At the end of the program they had decided to stay together and work things out.

Couple 2 - On one of the first seminars we conducted there was an inmate who was the assistant to the chaplain. He and his wife seemed to thoroughly enjoy the seminar. He was very impressed by the film "Fireproof" and was instrumental in getting one of the films follow up studies implemented into the unit with the chaplain. It was so encouraging to go back and see him as he continued to nurture his marriage and help the chaplain assist volunteers as various organizations presented their programs. He was looking forward to being released and going home. POP found out that he became ill and died unexpectedly. About a month later his son was tragically killed in an auto accident. His wife was a strong Christian but she had been hit very hard in a short period of time, losing both her husband and her son. Staff from POP attended the funeral of her son, and was encouraged to see a strong support group from her church had gathered around her.

On a lighter note, one Saturday morning as we pulled into the parking lot at Colorado City, Ron Brewer got out and started to unload the equipment. He pulled out the new black bags that we had just received to aid in transporting the Projector Screen and speaker tripod stands. Within 30 seconds a correctional officer pulled up, and demanded to know immediately what was in the black bags. It turns out that the control tower had spotted it and thought it was a big gun. Scared the dickens out of Ron!

One of the POP activities we did when the institution would allow it was to take a picture of the couple. At times it seemed to be a hassle and I questioned the importance of it. Was it really necessary? My question was answered when we received word that one of the participants in a seminar a few months before had a heart attack and died. When we contacted his wife to offer our condolences she shared with Ron that the last picture she had of her husband was the one that they took together with POP.

One Friday night as the women in one seminar sat around and got acquainted they were sharing some of the questions they were asked by people. The ladies were asking each other what they said when they were asked "What does your husband do?" (In reference to jobs) My favorite answer was given by a young woman who said, " I tell them that my husband works for the state." As all the ladies burst out laughing, they agreed that they had to remember that and use it.

One of the activities that POP used was to play the POP Marriage Game. It was a takeoff on the old TV show the "Dating Game". We would ask the couples questions and then each partner would write their answer on a note card. After completing all the questions we would put the couples next to each other and compare their answers. It was humorous to watch them as they interacted as husband and wife, laughing, and at times almost forgetting where they were.

Examples of questions were:

- What was your wife wearing the first time you met?
- What is your husband's favorite desert?
- What is your wife's favorite color?
- What cartoon character is your husband most like?
- What was the make and model of your husband's first car?
- Where is the strangest place you have ever slept?

One of the most memorable answers to where is the strangest place you have ever slept was shared by the couple who had gone to Goodwill to dump off an old couch. While they were trying to get the couch into the bin, she fell in, and couldn't get out. While he was trying to help her get out he fell in also. They yelled trying to get someone's attention to get them out, but they ended up sleeping in the bin on a pile of dirty clothes. Workers found them at the bottom of the bin the next morning.

At the bottom of the bin – have you been there? Are you there now? Have you jumped and jumped trying to crawl out, until you're exhausted? Have you yelled until you're hoarse trying to get someone's attention? Have you spent the night sleeping on a pile of dirty clothes at the bottom of the bin? <u>We all end up there at some point in our lives.</u> Just as the couple only needed some help – the workers who opened the lock on the door at the bottom of the bin helped them out. Not to oversimplify – the couples we have worked with the past four years, and the men that Stepping Stone continues to work with on a daily basis, as they are released from prison. They all need some help. It may be a simple phrase of encouragement, or simply a person who will look them in the eye and listen. You can't solve all their problems. You can't climb out of whatever situation they are in, and you are not God –you can't fix everything for them. By that I mean you are not the one is in control of their lives. God is, whether they recognize it or not. They still are allowed free will to make the choices. They can choose to turn their life around, and accept Him, or they can reject him. That is the simple choice God lets every person make.

But there are things you can do. You can offer the Love of Jesus to people who simply need to know that they are still loveable. They are still a person of value – to you, and to Christ. You can point them to the one who died for their sins, and loves them so much that he gave up his life for theirs. He is the one who offers them hope and a future. You can be Christ's "tangible hands and feet" on this earth reaching out to them.

IX.

A Season of Change

ON OCTOBER 1, 2011 the Federal Grant expired. We tried to find a way to sustain it, but each seminar cost between $7,000 - $10,000 , and giving for non-profits was down. We tried to find a way to keep it going: we submitted several proposals for grants, but unfortunately we were not selected. We talked about switching over and doing regular marriage seminars, but really our hearts were not there. After 3 months, staff members realized that it was time to start looking for jobs. *Sometimes, God's plan is for a season.* So, Ron went to work as a mud engineer in the oil field, Mindi worked a part time job for a frame shop and went on a mission trip to Israel, while I finally retired! Well, sort of, I have now taken over most of the correspondence for Stepping Stone, which entails quite an amount of paperwork & organization of folders. As my mother has reminded me she didn't read anywhere in the Bible anything about retiring. Then I couldn't shake that feeling that someone needed to write a book about the experiences we had had in the prisons. Believe me I talked to "Him" about this quite a bit. I reminded "Him" that I am not the talented, humorous one of the group, but I finally decided it was easier to write it than to point out all my weaknesses to Him. I think that He is finally getting through to me about obedience, and the fact is that it's His plan, and not mine that matters, really. I have found that while it was very easy for me to tell Clayton that he had better do what God impressed him to do, I seem to have a little more difficulty recognizing what "God's plan" for my life is. The one impression I have is to slow down, listen & read "His Word". Actually, I guess that's pretty good advice for all these days. Life just seems to move so fast that we forget to enjoy the moments.

One thing I know: Life is not a coincidence. There is a time and a season for everything. Paul Moore, who is a close friend of Steve Becker, and was a teacher for POP clearly illustrated that to me. One Saturday afternoon I was at the POP office working on a government report. The phone rang several times, and out of habit I picked it up and answered. Paul was on the other end of the line. He had called the POP office because it was the only number he could remember. Usually, no one was at the office on Saturday afternoons. Paul was in Guatemala. He had driven a bus deep into the interior of Central America to be delivered and used for ministry. He was hijacked. While lying in a ditch with a gun at his head, he witnessed to the young leader of the group. Paul had been hit in the head with the butt of a pistol, beaten pretty good, had his wallet taken with all cash, credit cards, passport, and cell phone stolen, but still he had witnessed. The young man had left Paul lying in the ditch and had not killed him after he had been told to.

Some would say it was just a coincidence that I was at the office that Saturday, that it was just a coincidence that the only number Paul could remember to call was the POP office, but I know that it wasn't a coincidence. I was right where God wanted me to be because I could talk to Paul on one phone while I reported everything to Steve Becker on my cell phone. They were able to connect and finish the mission. Some would say that Paul was lucky to have not been killed, but Paul would tell you about a peace that passes all understanding, and a rapport that he was able to establish with the young guerilla leader, not because of Paul, but because of God's presence in the midst of the situation. Paul would tell you about God being in complete control, and how if being killed would have been part of that plan, then he would have been in the presence of Jesus, immediately, and that would have been wonderful to him.

In Ecclesiastes 3:1 we are told that to everything there is a season. For a while we couldn't figure out why we didn't get another grant. After some months had passed we all began to realize that there was a season to the grant. It was an opportunity God gave us to be used by Him to show the couples, and the individuals God's Love and Grace in action reaching out to each of them. When it seemed to them as if no one cared, we were allowed to show them that God knew all about their situation, and He provided encouragement and love to them through ordinary people who didn't judge them but accepted them just as they were. If I have one regret it is that the knowledge, equipment, curriculum for Healthy Marriage Seminars and Fatherhood is no longer benefiting people who desperately need it. I know that it will be put to good use by Texas Arms of Love, but the incarcerated still need these types of programs.

This past week Clayton drove one of Stepping Stone's residents to a custody hearing concerning his child. Just two weeks earlier the young man and I had worked on a rent house together and over lunch he shared part of his past with me. It was one of those "God moments" where all is needed is for you to listen, and share some encouragement for the future. While incarcerated Steve-O had met Jesus Christ and the relationship had completely changed his life. One of his major concerns was to reestablish contact with his children and to someday be able to return home and live a true believer's life in front of his family. After returning home from the hearing, Clayton remarked to me that he had found out that Steve-O was the real deal. Clayton told me about overhearing Steve-O talking with his father. He told his father that he now had a relationship with Christ; to which his father replied, "That's good. I just hope you're not going to start preaching to me." Steve-O lovingly responded, "No dad, but I do want you to know that I'm concerned about you. I just don't want to be in heaven without you."

It is so wonderful to sit and talk with a recently released man who has come to know Christ. Many of them tell me that the greatest blessing was that they met Jesus while they were inside, and He has made all the difference! Stepping Stone receives anywhere from 60-90 inquiries a month concerning residency. In reviewing completed applications I have been amazed at the number that say they met Christ while incarcerated and that meeting Him was worth the price of incarceration.

I believe that in today's society the incarcerated are viewed similar to the "lepers" in Jesus time. People just live their lives ignoring them. We act like they don't exist. Really, I think that we are scared of them. Just as people in Biblical times were scared that they would get leprosy and would not go near the leper, we are afraid. We are afraid that what they have might rub off on us. The interesting truth is that we already have what they have. We are all sinners, and God loved us and died for us while we were dirty. Many of the people we met believed that they had to clean up before they could go to church or come to Christ. They had trouble believing that Jesus loved them just as they were because they cannot see what He can see. He can see the person they can become when they are filled with His Love and Hope.

I must say that while this was not the ministry that I envisioned being called to, what I have found is that it is a great blessing to be a part of God's plan to change lives and make new creations. What an incredible ministry it is! Prison Ministry has allowed me to see the miracles that God's Love and Power accomplishes in the darkest of places. He is amazing! Actually, I can't wait to see what the next part of the adventure holds or what He has planned for the next season.

Psalm 138:8 The Lord will fulfill His purpose for me.

Printed in the United States
By Bookmasters